MW00760946

H.E.L.P., Harmony and Happiness
My Journey of Transformation

Name:
_____

I am ready to create harmony in my life.

*Whatever reason you have for not being
"somebody", there's somebody who had
the same problem and overcame it.*

Barbara Reynolds

Copyright ©2017 by Andrea D. Merriman

All rights reserved. This book or any portion thereof may not be reproduced or used in any manner whatsoever without the express written permission of the publisher except for the use of brief quotations in a book review and certain other non-commercial uses permitted by copyright law.

Printed in the United States of America

First Printing, 2017

This book is not intended as a substitute for the medical advice of physicians. The reader should regularly consult a physician in matters relating to his/her health and particularly with respect to any symptoms that may require diagnosis or medical attention.

Dedication

This book is dedicated to my family and friends, especially my daughters, Grace, Julia and Philadelphia who have believed and supported me through it all.

In Memory of...

This journal was inspired by my journey of transformation after the death of my daughters, Lois and Jennifer, who are awaiting the time that we will meet again.

Proceeds from the sales of this journal will be used to help domestic violence survivors and youth learn skills to live in healthy relationships. The Jennifer Y. Merriman H.E.L.P. Program© and the Jennifer Y. Merriman H.E.L.P. Teens Talk©, both offer Hope, Empowerment, Life Skills and Prevention methods to women from their youth through adulthood.

http://jymhelpprogram.com

This journal is for you if you are ready for change

and to be the best form of you.

This is your personal space to express your thoughts on

your journey that leads to your glory.

I have included a few quotes that helped me forward.

Blank boxes have been included so you can catalog your

inspirational quotes and highlight them for easy access.

At any time during this journey, you are welcome to reach

out and ask a question or share a thought.

Email admin@andreadmerriman.net

or connect on social media @HarmonyCoachAndrea

Thank you for allowing me to be a part of your journey as

you become the ultimate you in harmony.

Andrea D. Merriman

Today is the beginning… Create Self-Harmony

Invasive dialogue from the mind's own heart

Elevate it says

Alleviate pain's thoughts

Thou the path seems rigid

Appears complex and breeds cries

Peace is at the crossroads

Set apart from the lies

Set foot towards the light

Let the dark remain in shadows

Harmonize with life

Place doubt in your sorrows

Uplift oneself

From within groom your power

For the time will approach when you need that inner ladder.
~Mary Guy

Harmony is Within Your Reach

Hi, I'm Creative Harmony Coach Andrea D. Merriman, I am the CEO and founder of The Merriman Resource Center and Feminine Life Rebuilders. My mission is to help you find relief. If you are stressed, unorganized or struggling to stay focused because you are doing too much, journaling will help.

Have you ever thought, *"if I could only find balance, things would be better?"* In my opinion, balance is a fantasy. It is near impossible to spend an equal amount of time in each area of your life. There are 24 hours in a day. We have been told to spend eight hours sleeping and we use eight hours working. Which only leaves eight hours for family, friends and other social tasks. Trying to divide eight hours between each of these areas can be stressful, frustrating and downright discouraging. The theory of work and life balance has left us in a stressed-out bundle of nerves seeking peaceful bliss.

What you need is harmony. Harmony can give you relief. It can cause that *"AHA"* moment when you know everything could be ok. Harmony is Hope with a plan. Creative Harmony is hope with a plan, peace and a path to becoming the Ultimate You.

This journal was created as a tool for you to use with the Clarity and Empowerment programs I provide to my clients, (*Check out my website for a list of programs:* www.andreadmerriman.net). However, it can also be used as a standalone product.

The key to making this journal work for you is simple; use it. Be consistent. Dream big. Dreams that motivate you when times are tough. Dreams that give you a purpose in life. Set goals that are so strong you are willing to fight for them. Let your goals and dreams be your mission in life. Be true to yourself and your mission. If you need help, reach out and ask. There is someone ready to collaborate and help you reach your goals.

Use this journal for your personal, professional and spiritual life. Use it to map out your future and to record the history in the making called the present.

Create the Harmony You Deserve

I used to work diligently to bring balance to my life. The more I tried, the more things became unbalanced. After years of trying, I learned what worked best for me. I started using list, setting goals, and scheduling in time for all things, not just appointments. As a result, I discovered harmony. I discovered, to make things work for my life I had to do things differently. I had to create my own harmony. I did things like setting one day a week as movie night with the kids. I recorded the kids school schedule in my planner for the year. This helped me when planning trips and vacations. Each week I reviewed the week ahead with my family. This allowed us to be on one accord. I also scheduled in time for work and self. This journal was created as a by-product of my harmony journey. I am sure it will help you.

When your thoughts keep you stuck and your heart feels full, journal. To make this work, don't spend so much time planning that you never act. There may be times when you want to make things perfect before moving forward, instead I encourage you to think things through, then move forward.

As a mission focused woman, you may be looking for ways to serve others. Inserting yourself into this equation may seem a bit overwhelming. In those times, journal. Get your thoughts out on paper. Make this journal the blueprint of your success. There are times when you must keep moving even when there is fear. I think of fear as, **F**uel to **E**mpower you to use **A**ll your **R**esources. Don't let fear keep you from creating harmony and happiness in your life.

According to the *(National Women's Business Council, 2012)* 89.5% of women owned businesses are sole-proprietorships and generated 229.2 billion dollars. This means that you may be carrying a heavy weight. You must create a plan that works for you.

A plan that embraces your goals and life to allow you to be successful, by your terms. It may not look like the next persons way of doing it, but it is what makes your life peaceful and productive. That is why I encourage Creative Harmony.

Think out of the box and create a plan that is a positive flow with your mind, body and spirit. Overall, women owned businesses generated over 1.6 trillion dollars in 2012 *(National Women's Business Council, 2012)* Many women are doing this and handling other responsibilities.

You may spend the day being an executive, wife, mother, daughter, grandmother or best friend. This can leave you feeling exhausted, run down, stressed, or plain tired. By the end of the day your mind may be reeling yet too cloudy to process priorities properly. There may be times when you can't see the light at the end of the tunnel. You may even feel at times like your pain will consume you. Don't give up, use the worksheets and journaling space provided to help you discover the driving force that will put your life in sync and create a positive energy flow for you. Stay on your path because harmony and happiness are within your reach.

Start each Journey with a Road Map

List the top 10 things you want to achieve. It may be spiritual, family goals, career goals or personal goals. Visualize what things would look like, feel like and how it would affect you. Stretch your mind and dream again.

Underneath that list write the top 3 things you want to achieve for yourself in the next 6 -12 months. Dream big but keep them realistic.

Dreams/Visions/Goals

1. _____

2. _____

3. _____

4. _____

5. _____

6. _____

7. _____

8. _____

9. _____

10. _____

In Six Months	1. _____
	2. _____
	3. _____

I need to schedule time for…

Meditation: _____   Notes:

Exercise: _____

Family: _____

Business: _____

Work: _____

Finances: _____

Housework: _____

_____

_____

I want to make it happen by:

_____

Be Realistic

Be realistic about how you are spending your time. Don't let the day go by and time is wasted. Be a good steward of your time.

Being successful takes time, commitment, consistency and perseverance. Be aware of your time wasters.
For 5-7 days do the following to see where your time is going:

- Write down the tasks you completed each day.
- Write and circle the task you "wanted" to complete and did not.
- Critique your progress by journaling.
- Identify the things you can change to help reach your goals. Highlight the things you continue doing. Each day you should be moving forward and reaching your goals.

Daily Tasks

Daily Tasks

Eliminate the Negative

Distractions will keep you running around in circles. They can be notifications on your phone, phone calls, noise from outside the window or a person demanding your attention often. It is important as you start creating harmony in your life you prepare to reduce distractions. Eliminate them entirely as you deem necessary. Especially people who are very demanding or not flexible to your needs. When you allow others to set the tone of your day your goals may not be met.

After you critique your daily tasks, identify distractions. Find out what they are and make a note to eliminate them. Also, when setting goals, set specific times to allow distractions. No matter the amount of planning, there will always be something unexpected happen, do what works for you and don't be discouraged. Remember you are creating harmony in your life.

Distractions

Distractions

It is Your Life

It is your life. Own it. Keep your sacred moments. Embrace your fears and make them work for you. Roll with the punches and stand up fighting. Meaning you may have to embrace your fears or acknowledge pain you have tried to hide. You can't push through the pain unless you acknowledge it is there. Remember the fear that is holding you back is really the fuel you need to move forward. Discover the resources available to you and use them to help you keep your head up. Then create a safe-haven for your strength and well-being to grow.

That safe-haven may be inside you. It may be your confidence, drive and you building your spiritual awareness and faith. It may be your environment. You may find a safe place to journal, pray, meditate or relax. It may be in your relationships. Find an accountability partner. Journal together. Start a group of journaling friends that meet monthly or weekly and discuss your experiences. Incorporate one or all of the above. Just Stop, Step and Glow.

STOP. STEP. GLOW

STOP living the life others have set for you. Stop sabotaging yourself. Stop selling yourself short. Stop the negative chatter inside your head. Stop allowing the negative chatter from others dictate who you are and who you can become.

STEP into your greatness. Step into the Spiritual being you want to be. Step into the abundant life you dreamed of. Step past your trauma and pain. Step into your fears and crush them. Step in the room and own it.

GLOW with the passion for your mission. Glow in the radiance of your inner beauty. Glow in your achievements. Glow in your harmony. Let the Journaling Begin…

If you don't build your dreams, someone will hire you to build theirs. Unknown

Strength and Honor are her clothing: and she shall rejoice in time to come. Proverbs 31:25 KJV

She openeth her mouth with wisdom: and her tongue is the law of kindness. Proverbs 31:26 KJV

We must have change in order to survive. Pearl Bailey

Today is the beginning… Create Self-Harmony

Today is the beginning… Create Self-Harmony

Today is the beginning… Create Self-Harmony

Today is the beginning… Create Self-Harmony

Today is the beginning… Create Self-Harmony

Today is the beginning... Create Self-Harmony

Today is the beginning… Create Self-Harmony

Today is the beginning… Create Self-Harmony

Today is the beginning… Create Self-Harmony

Today is the beginning… Create Self-Harmony

Today is the beginning... Create Self-Harmony

Today is the beginning… Create Self-Harmony

Today is the beginning… Create Self-Harmony

Today is the beginning… Create Self-Harmony

Today is the beginning… Create Self-Harmony

Today is the beginning… Create Self-Harmony

Today is the beginning... Create Self-Harmony

Today is the beginning… Create Self-Harmony

Today is the beginning... Create Self-Harmony

Today is the beginning… Create Self-Harmony

Today is the beginning… Create Self-Harmony

Today is the beginning… Create Self-Harmony

Today is the beginning… Create Self-Harmony

Today is the beginning… Create Self-Harmony

Today is the beginning… Create Self-Harmony

Today is the beginning… Create Self-Harmony

Today is the beginning… Create Self-Harmony

Today is the beginning… Create Self-Harmony

Today is the beginning… Create Self-Harmony

Today is the beginning… Create Self-Harmony

Today is the beginning... Create Self-Harmony

Today is the beginning… Create Self-Harmony

Today is the beginning… Create Self-Harmony

Today is the beginning… Create Self-Harmony

Today is the beginning… Create Self-Harmony

Today is the beginning… Create Self-Harmony

Today is the beginning… Create Self-Harmony

Today is the beginning... Create Self-Harmony

Today is the beginning... Create Self-Harmony

Today is the beginning… Create Self-Harmony

Today is the beginning… Create Self-Harmony

Today is the beginning… Create Self-Harmony

Today is the beginning... Create Self-Harmony

Today is the beginning… Create Self-Harmony

Andrea D. Merriman

Wife, Mother, Trainer, Transformational Speaker,
Creative Harmony Coach and Advocate for Life Ownership

Creator of:

Andrea D. Merriman, LLC

Jennifer Y. Merriman H.E.L.P. Program©

Jennifer Y. Merriman H.E.L.P. Teens Talk©

Website: www.andreadmerriman.net

Email: admin@andreadmerriman.net

90284583R00139

Made in the USA
Columbia, SC
28 February 2018